Understanding God's Restoration Mandate

"For God so loved the world that he gave his only begotten Son, that whosoever believeth in him should not perish, but have everlasting life."

John 3:16

by

Franklin N. Abazie

Understanding God's Restoration Mandate

COPYRIGHT 2019 *by* Franklin N Abazie
ISBN: 978-0-9966-263-9-2

All right reserved. This book or any portion thereof may not be reproduced or used in any manner whatsoever without the express written permission of the publisher, except for the use of brief quotations in a book review. All Bible quotes are from King James Version and others as noted.

Published by:
F N ABAZIE PUBLISHING HOUSE---a.k.a, Empowerment Bookstore:

That I may publish with the voice of thanksgiving and tell of all thy wondrous works.
Psalms26:7

To order additional copies, wholesales or booking:
Call the Church office (973-372-7518)
or Empowerment Bookstore Hotline 973-393-8518

Worship address:
343 Sanford Avenue Newark New Jersey 07106
Administrative Head Office address:
33 Schley Street Newark New Jersey 07112
Email:pastorfranknto@yahoo.com
Website www.fnabaziehealingministries.org
Publishing House: www.fnabaziepublishinghouse.org

This book is a production of F N Abazie Publishing House. A publication Arms of Miracle of God Ministries 2019
Revised Edition

CONTENTS

The Mandate of The Commission iv

Arms of The Commission v

Favor Confession vi

Introduction viii

CHAPTER 1
God's Covenant of Abundance Life 71

CHAPTER 2
God Precious Promises 91

CHAPTER 4
Prayer of Salvation 139

CHAPTER 4
About The Author 148

Books By Rev Franklin N Abazie 151

Understanding God's Restoration Mandate

THE MANDATE OF THE COMMISSION

"THE MOMENT IS DUE TO IMPACT YOUR WORLD THROUGH THE REVIVAL OF THE HEALING & MIRACLE MINISTRY OF JESUS CHRIST OF NAZARETH."

"I AM SENDING YOU TO RESTORE HEALTH UNTO THEE AND I WILL HEAL THEE OF THY WOUNDS, SAID THE LORD OF HOST."

ARMS OF THE COMMISSION

1) F N Abazie Ministries-Miracle of God Ministries (Miracle Chapel Intl)
2) F N Abazie TV Ministries: Global Television Ministry Outreach.
3) F N Abazie Radio Ministries: Radio Broadcasting Outreach.
4) F N Abazie Publishing House: Book Publication.
5) F N Abazie Bible School: also called Word of Healing Bible School (W.O.H.B.S)
6) F N Abazie Evangelistic Ass: Miracle of God Ministries: Global Crusade
7) Empowerment Bookstore: Book distribution.
8) F N Abazie Helping Hands: Meeting the help of the needy world wide
9) F N Abazie Disaster Recovery Mission: Global Disaster Recovery.
10) F N Abazie Prison Ministry: Prison Ministry for all convicts "Second chance"

Some of our ministry arms are waiting the appointed time to commence.

FAVOR CONFESSION

Father thank you for making me righteous and accepted through the blood of Jesus Christ. Because of that, I am blessed and highly favored by God. I am the subject of your affection. Your favor surrounds me as a shield, and the first thing that people see around me is your favored shield.

Thank you that I have favor with you and man today. All day long people go out of their way to bless me and help me. I have favor with everyone that I deal with today. Doors that were once closed are now opened for me. I receive preferential treatment, and I have special privileges, I am Gods favored child.

No good thing will he withhold from me. Because of Gods favor my enemies cannot triumph over my life. I have supernatural increase and promotion. I declare restoration to everything that the devil has

Favor Confession

stolen from my life. I have honor in the midst of my adversaries and an increase in assets, especially in real estate and expansion of territories.

Because I am highly favored by God, I experience great victories, supernatural turnarounds, and miraculous breakthrough in the midst of great impossibilities. I receive recognition, prominence, and honor. Petitions are granted to me even by ungodly authorities. Policies, rules, regulations, and laws are changed and reverse on my behalf.

I win battles that I don't even have to fight, because God fights them for me. This is the day, the set time and the designated moment for me to experience the free favor of God, that profusely and lavishly abound on my behalf in Jesus name. **Amen.**

Understanding God's Restoration Mandate

INTRODUCTION

"Restore unto me the joy of thy salvation; and uphold me with thy free spirit."

Psalms 51:12

"And *I will restore to you* the years that the locust hath eaten, the cankerworm, and the caterpiller, and the palmerworm, my great army which I sent among you." Joel 2:25

I believe *whatever we lost as a result of the fall of man,* God will *restore it* into our lives. For unless we *understand God's restoration mandate* we will miss what belongs to us in life. It is written *"Ask of me, and I shall give thee the heathen for thine inheritance, and the uttermost parts of the earth for thy possession."* Psalms 2:8

Introduction

"….. For this purpose the Son of God was manifested, that he might destroy the works of the devil." 1John3:8

"I am come that they might have life, and that they might have it more abundantly." John10:10.

I have written this book, because I believe God is restoring our lives in this end time generation. In fact whole reason for the gospel of Jesus Christ is for our "RESTORATION". I see God restoring your marriage. I see God restoring your business. I see God restoring your finances.

Come with me let's examine together what the Holy Ghost is saying about God's plan to restore the life of man.

Happy Reading!

HIS DESTINY WAS THE CROSS....

HIS PURPOSE WAS LOVE....

HIS REASON WAS YOU....

"For a just man falleth seven times, and riseth up again: but the wicked shall fall into mischief."

Proverb24:16

"And said to his servant, Go up now, look toward the sea. And he went up, and looked, and said, There is nothing. And he said, Go again seven times."

1king18:43

"And it came to pass at the seventh time, that he said, Behold, there ariseth a little cloud out of the sea, like a man's hand. And he said, Go up, say unto Ahab, Prepare thy chariot, and get thee down that the rain stop thee not."

1king18:44

"Then He got up and left the synagogue, and entered Simon's home Now Simon's mother-in-law was suffering from a high fever, and they asked Him to help her. And standing over her, He rebuked the fever, and it left her; and she immediately got up and waited on them."

Luke 4:38-39

"And a woman who had a hemorrhage for twelve years, and could not be healed by anyone, came up behind Him and touched the fringe of His cloak, and immediately her hemorrhage stopped."

Luke 8:43-44

"And there in front of Him was a man suffering from dropsy. And Jesus answered and spoke to the lawyers and Pharisees, saying, "Is it lawful to heal on the Sabbath, or not?" But they kept silent. And He took hold of him and healed him, and sent him away."

Luke 14:2-4

"Soon afterwards He went to a city called Nain; and His disciples were going along with Him, accompanied by a large crowd. Now as He approached the gate of the city, a dead man was being carried out, the only son of his mother, and she was a widow; and a sizeable crowd from the city was with her. When the Lord saw her, He felt compassion for her, and said to her, "Do not weep."

Luke 7:11-15

"Yet even now," declares the LORD, "Return to Me with all your heart, And with fasting, weeping and mourning;"

Joel2:12-13

"Whom heaven must receive until the period of restoration of all things about which God spoke by the mouth of His holy prophets from ancient time."

Acts3:21

"Now a certain man was sick, Lazarus of Bethany, the village of Mary and her sister Martha. It was the Mary who anointed the Lord with ointment, and wiped His feet with her hair, whose brother Lazarus was sick. So the sisters sent word to Him, saying,

"Lord, behold, he whom You love is sick."

John 11:1-44

"And they came to Bethsaida And they brought a blind man to Jesus and implored Him to touch him. Taking the blind man by the hand, He brought him out of the village; and after spitting on his eyes and laying His hands on him, He asked him, "Do you see anything?" And he looked up and said, "I see men, for I see them like trees, walking around."

Mark8:22-25

"As He passed by, He saw a man blind from birth. And His disciples asked Him, "Rabbi, who sinned, this man or his parents, that he would be born blind?" Jesus answered, "It was neither that this man sinned, nor his parents; but it was so that the works of God might be displayed in him."

John 9:1-7

"They brought to Him one who was deaf and spoke with difficulty, and they implored Him to lay His hand on him. Jesus took him aside from the crowd, by himself, and put His fingers into his ears, and after spitting, He touched his tongue with the saliva; and looking up to heaven with a deep sigh, He said to him, "Ephphatha!" that is, "Be opened."

Mark7:32-35

"And the wolf will dwell with the lamb, And the leopard will lie down with the young goat, And the calf and the young lion and the fatling together; And a little boy will lead them. Also the cow and the bear will graze, Their young will lie down together, And the lion will eat straw like the ox. The nursing child will play by the hole of the cobra, And the weaned child will put his hand on the viper's den."

Isaiah11:6-9

"The afflicted and needy are seeking water, but there is none, And their tongue is parched with thirst; I, the LORD, will answer them Myself, As the God of Israel I will not forsake them. "I will open rivers on the bare heights And springs in the midst of the valleys; I will make the wilderness a pool of water And the dry land fountains of water. "I will put the cedar in the wilderness, The acacia and the myrtle and the olive tree; I will place the juniper in the desert Together with the box tree and the cypress."

Isaiah 41:17-20

"For as the rain and the snow come down from heaven, And do not return there without watering the earth And making it bear and sprout, And furnishing seed to the sower and bread to the eater; So will My word be which goes forth from My mouth; It will not return to Me empty, Without accomplishing what I desire, And without succeeding in the matter for which I sent it. For you will go out with joy And be led forth with peace; The mountains and the hills will break forth into shouts of joy before you, And all the trees of the field will clap their hands."

Isaiah55:10-11

"Then I saw a new heaven and a new earth; for the first heaven and the first earth passed away, and there is no longer any sea. And I saw the holy city, new Jerusalem, coming down out of heaven from God, made ready as a bride adorned for her husband. And I heard a loud voice from the throne, saying, "Behold, the tabernacle of God is among men, and He will dwell among them, and they shall be His people, and God Himself will be among them."

Rev21:1-4

"Then he showed me a river of the water of life, clear as crystal, coming from the throne of God and of the Lamb, in the middle of its street On either side of the river was the tree of life, bearing twelve kinds of fruit, yielding its fruit every month; and the leaves of the tree were for the healing of the nations. There will no longer be any curse; and the throne of God and of the Lamb will be in it, and His bond-servants will serve Him."

Rev22:1-5

"Oh, that the salvation of Israel would come out of Zion! When the LORD restores His captive people, Jacob will rejoice, Israel will be glad."

Psalms 14:7

"For God will save Zion and build the cities of Judah, That they may dwell there and possess it. The descendants of His servants will inherit it, And those who love His name will dwell in it."

Psalm 69:35-36

"For I am the LORD your God, who upholds your right hand, Who says to you, 'Do not fear, I will help you."

Isaiah 41:13

"Listen to me, you who pursue righteousness, Who seek the LORD: Look to the rock from which you were hewn And to the quarry from which you were dug. Look to Abraham your father And to Sarah who gave birth to you in pain; When he was but one I called him, Then I blessed him and multiplied him." Indeed, the LORD will comfort Zion; He will comfort all her waste places And her wilderness He will make like Eden, And her desert like the garden of the LORD; Joy and gladness will be found in her, Thanksgiving and sound of a melody."

Isaiah51:1-6

"Thus says the LORD, 'Behold, I will restore the fortunes of the tents of Jacob And have compassion on his dwelling places; And the city will be rebuilt on its ruin, And the palace will stand on its rightful place. From them will proceed thanksgiving And the voice of those who celebrate; And I will multiply them and they will not be diminished; I will also honor them and they will not be insignificant. 'Their children also will be as formerly, And their congregation shall be established before Me; And I will punish all their oppressors."

Jeremiah 30:18-22

"But you, O mountains of Israel, you will put forth your branches and bear your fruit for My people Israel; for they will soon come. 'For, behold, I am for you, and I will turn to you, and you will be cultivated and sown. 'I will multiply men on you, all the house of Israel, all of it; and the cities will be inhabited and the waste places will be rebuilt."

Ezekiel 36:8-12

"Behold, days are coming," declares the LORD, "When the plowman will overtake the reaper And the treader of grapes him who sows seed; When the mountains will drip sweet wine And all the hills will be dissolved. "Also I will restore the captivity of My people Israel, And they will rebuild the ruined cities and live in them; They will also plant vineyards and drink their wine, And make gardens and eat their fruit. "I will also plant them on their land, And they will not again be rooted out from their land Which I have given them," Says the LORD your God."

Amos9:13-15

"Within three more days Pharaoh will lift up your head and restore you to your office; and you will put Pharaoh's cup into his hand according to your former custom when you were his cupbearer."

Genesis 40:13

"If you are pure and upright, Surely now He would rouse Himself for you And restore your righteous estate."

Job 8:6

"Nevertheless, I will restore their captivity, the captivity of Sodom and her daughters, the captivity of Samaria and her daughters, and along with them your own captivity."

Ezekiel 16:53

"Now it came about after this that Joash decided to restore the house of the LORD."
   2Chronicle24:4

"Then we asked those elders and said to them thus, 'Who issued you a decree to rebuild this temple and to finish this structure?"

Ezra 5:9

"Then David defeated Hadadezer, the son of Rehob king of Zobah, as he went to restore his rule at the River."

2samuel8:3

"But afterward I will restore The fortunes of the sons of Ammon," Declares the LORD."

Jeremiah49:6

"Return, O faithless sons, I will heal your faithlessness." "Behold, we come to You; For You are the LORD our God."

Jeremiah3:22

"I will heal their apostasy, I will love them freely, For My anger has turned away from them."

Hosea 14:4

"He will again have compassion on us; He will tread our iniquities under foot Yes, You will cast all their sins Into the depths of the sea."

Micah 7:19

"I have seen his ways, but I will heal him; I will lead him and restore comfort to him and to his mourners."

Isaiah 57:18

*"For I will restore you to health
And I will heal you of your
wounds,' declares the LORD,
'Because they have called
you an outcast, saying: "It is
Zion; no one cares for her."*

Jeremiah30:17

"But I keep under my body, and bring it into subjection: lest that by any means, when I have preached to others, I myself should be a castaway."

1cor9:27

"I must work the works of him that sent me, while it is day: the night cometh, when no man can work."

John9:4

"Whoever spares the rod hates his son, but he who loves him is diligent to discipline him."
Proverb13:24

"Those whom I love, I reprove and discipline, so be zealous and repent."

Revelation 3:19

"The rod and reproof give wisdom, but a child left to himself brings shame to his mother."

Proverb29:15

> *"So he fed them according to the integrity of his heart; and guided them by the skilfulness of his hands."*
>
> **Psalm 78:72**

"And ye have forgotten the exhortation which speaketh unto you as unto children, My son, despise not thou the chastening of the Lord, nor faint when thou art rebuked of him:"

Hebrews 12:5

"For whom the Lord loveth he chasteneth, and scourgeth every son whom he receiveth."

Hebrews12:6

"If ye endure chastening, God dealeth with you as with sons; for what son is he whom the father chasteneth not"?

Hebrews12:7

"But if ye be without chastisement, whereof all are partakers, then are ye bastards, and not sons."

Hebrews 12:8

"Furthermore we have had fathers of our flesh which corrected us, and we gave them reverence: shall we not much rather be in subjection unto the Father of spirits, and live?"

Hebrews 12:9

"He that spareth his rod hateth his son: but he that loveth him chasteneth him betimes."

Proverb13:24

"Let thy work appear unto thy servants, and thy glory unto their children."

Psalm 90:16

"And let the beauty of the Lord our God be upon us: and establish thou the work of our hands upon us; yea, the work of our hands establish thou it."

Psalm 90:17

"And he shall be like a tree planted by the rivers of water, that bringeth forth his fruit in his season; his leaf also shall not wither; and whatsoever he doeth shall prosper."

Psalm 1:3

"I must work the works of him that sent me, while it is day: the night cometh, when no man can work."

John9:4

"For even when we were with you, this we commanded you, that if any would not work, neither should he eat."

2theo3:10

"And that ye study to be quiet, and to do your own business, and to work with your own hands, as we commanded you;

1theo4:11

"To discipline a child produces wisdom, but a mother is disgraced by an undisciplined child."

Proverbs 29:15

"Whoever loves discipline loves knowledge, but whoever hates correction is stupid."

Proverbs 12:1

"Blessed is the one whom God corrects; so do not despise the discipline of the Almighty."

Job 5:17

"Blessed is the one you discipline, LORD, the one you teach from your law;"

Psalm 94:12

> *"But Jesus answered them, My Father worketh hitherto, and I work".*
> **John 5:17**

CHAPTER 1
GOD'S COVENANT OF ABUNDANCE LIFE

"The thief cometh not, but for to steal, and to kill, and to destroy: I am come that they might have life, and that they might have it more abundantly."

John 10:10

It is in God's *redemptive plan to save us from our sins* and to bless us more *abundantly*. The word says "The thief cometh not, but for to steal, and to kill, and to destroy: I am come that they might have life, and that they might have it more abundantly."

Understanding God's Restoration Mandate

Our God is a God of covenant. *"I have made a covenant with my chosen, I have sworn unto David my servant,"* **Psalm 89:3**

"My covenant will I not break, nor alter the thing that is gone out of my lips." **Psalm 89:34** In my own opinion, I believe that money, property, relationship lost can be restored. *But time lost can never be restored is time.*

"I will restore the years that the locust has eaten" (Joel 2:25). It is the *will of God to restore* our lives more abundantly. I encourage you, *whatever you lost in time past God is going to restore it into* your life.

The covenant of abundance is among the testimonies of the power of the gospel. As a believer, we must be expectant of God's *covenant of abundance.* If you have never experienced it I will encourage you to be in expectant of it. The word of God says *"....the abundance of the sea shall*

CHAPTER 1 : God's Covenant of Abundance life

be converted unto thee, the forces of the Gentiles shall come unto thee." **Isaiah 60:5**

WHAT ELSE WILL GOD RESTORE?

---God will restore lost years of hardship and difficulty-----

God wants to grant us supernatural favor. God is sending a onetime favor that will erase our life time labor in this season. *"Thou shalt arise, and have mercy upon Zion: for the time to favour her, yea, the set time, is come."* **Psalm 102:13**

God will restore every lost time of hardship in our lives. *"...and I will settle you after your old estates, and will do better unto you than at your beginnings: and ye shall know that I am the Lord."* **Ezekiel 36:11** God will restore your wasted years of suffering and pain.

Understanding God's Restoration Mandate

The Lord told me that He is doing a new thing on earth. All those painful years of sorrow and tears, God is compensating you in this season. *I'm talking to those who have lost businesses, finances, and a loved one.* If you have never been through pain, you cannot counsel someone in pain. God is going to restore your life.

Lost years are loveless years

Often strive and division comes to a family, alienating loved ones. Children grow up, and those years cannot be recovered. A marriage *quietly endures in* which love has been burning low for many years.

You see a couple who are really in love, and you say, "I wish I could be loved like that." Or you have not yet met the person you would like to meet. It feels like the years are moving on. You can never get them back. The locusts have eaten them.

CHAPTER 1 : God's Covenant of Abundance life

Lost years are rebellious years

Perhaps you grew up with many blessings, but in your heart you wanted to rebel. You didn't fully understand this urge, but you gave yourself to it. Instead of bringing you pleasure, rebellion brought you pain. Now you look back on those years with regret, the years that the locusts have eaten.

Lost years are misdirected years

The path you chose in your career or at college was a dead end. You just didn't fit. Often in your mind, and sometimes in your conversation, you say, "How did I end up here? If only.... If only I had made that move.... If only I had taken that opportunity.... If only I had chosen a different path." But the moment has passed. It's gone. You can't go back to it. You're left with locust years.

Understanding God's Restoration Mandate

Lost years are Christ-less years

All Christ-less years are locust years. This point is worth thinking about if you have not yet made a commitment to Christ. Ask anyone who came to faith in Christ later in life, and they will tell you that they wish they'd come to Christ sooner than they did: "How much foolishness I would have avoided. How much more good might have been done through my life."

How does God Restores Lost Years?

Take heart! There is hope, because God can restore your lost, locust years. He does so in three ways.

God can restore lost years by deepening your communion with Christ.

"You shall know that I am in the midst of Israel, and that I am the Lord your God" (Joel 2:27). These people, who have endured

CHAPTER 1 : God's Covenant of Abundance life

so much, enjoy a communion with the Lord that is far greater than anything they had ever known before in their religious lives. Christ can restore lost years by deepening your fellowship with him.

Why not ask him for this?

Tell him, "Lord, I have spent too many years without you, too many years at a distance from you. *Fill my heart with love and gratitude for Christ.* Let the loss of these years make my love for Christ greater than it would ever have been. Restore to me the years the locusts have eaten. "

God can restore lost years by multiplying your fruitfulness.

The harvests for these people had been wiped out for four years, but God restored the years that the locusts had eaten by giving bumper harvests. This provision makes me think about the parable where Jesus spoke about a harvest that could be 30-, 60-, or

100-fold. There's a huge difference between these three harvests. Three years at 100-fold is as much fruit as a decade at 30-fold.

Why not ask him for this?

"Lord, the locusts have eaten too many years of our lives. You have called us as your disciples to bear fruit that will last. Too many fruitless years have passed. Now Lord, we ask of you, give us some years now in which more lasting fruit will be born than in all of our years of small harvests."

God can restore lost years by bringing long-term gain from short-term loss.

The effect of these great trials in your life will be that "the tested genuineness of your faith . . . may result in praise and glory and honor at the revelation of Jesus Christ" (1 Peter 1:7). The praise, glory, and honor go to Christ because his power guarded you and kept you through the hardest years of your life.

CHAPTER 1 : God's Covenant of Abundance life

Thinking about "years that the locust has eaten," years that have been taken, I think of something Isaiah said about our Lord Jesus: "He was cut off out of the land of the living" (Isaiah 53:8).

Here was the Lord Jesus in the prime of life. He was three years into his ministry at 33 years old. You would think that a man launching a new enterprise at the age of 33 has everything in front of him. But Isaiah says, "He was cut off." He was cut off because he came under the judgment of God, not for his own sins—because he had none—but for ours.

Our sins, our grief, our sorrows, were laid on him. Our judgment fell on him. Our locusts swarmed all over him. The life of God's tender shoot was "cut off." Then, on the third day, the Son of God rose in the power of an eternal life. He offers himself to you, and he says what no one else can ever say: "I will restore the years that the locusts have eaten."

You may have been through some trouble, but God is the One Who brings restoration.

Isaiah 61:7 says, "For your shame ye shall have double; and for confusion they shall rejoice in their portion: therefore in their land they shall possess the double: everlasting joy shall be unto them."

In The Amplified Bible, this verse says, ". . . You shall have a twofold RECOMPENSE. . . ." The word recompense is the same word that we get worker's compensation from. You know what worker's compensation is for? If you get injured on the job, they pay you worker's compensation.

God is saying, "You're working for Me. You got hurt in the service of the Lord. And I'm going to give you worker's

CHAPTER 1 : God's Covenant of Abundance life

compensation. I'm going to give you double for your trouble." Glory to God!

If I may say this, the life and well-being of the believer is in the hands of God like a bow and arrow in the hands of an archer. The truth is, no matter what the enemy will throw at us, we are more than conqueror through Christ. It is written *"Nay, in all these things we are more than conquerors through him that loved us."* **Romans8:37**

"What shall we then say to these things? If God be for us, who can be against us?" **Romans8:31**

"Ye are of God, little children, and have overcome them: because greater is he that is in you, than he that is in the world." **1John4:4**

"For whatsoever is born of God overcometh the world: and this is the victory that overcometh the world, even our faith." **1John5:4**

"And he said unto them, Ye are from beneath; I am from above: ye are of this world; I am not of this world." **John8:23**

"And he answered, Fear not: for they that be with us are more than they that be with them." **2King6:16**

"He that cometh from above is above all: he that is of the earth is earthly, and speaketh of the earth: he that cometh from heaven is above all." **John3:31**

"And hath raised us up together, and made us sit together in heavenly places in Christ Jesus". **Ephesians2:6**

How do I Resist the devil?

---- *"Submit yourselves therefore to God. Resist the devil, and he will flee from you."* **James4:7**

"Whatever you do not want in life, we must never watch nor tolerate them." For

CHAPTER 1 : God's Covenant of Abundance life

unless we resist the devil, he will not flea away from us. It is written "Know ye not, that to whom ye yield yourselves servants to obey, his servants ye are to whom ye obey; whether of sin unto death, or of obedience unto righteousness?" Romans 6:16

----*"neither be ye sorry; for the joy of the Lord is your strength."* **Neh8:10**

It is easy to make up excuses, and complain in life. For unless we *make the joy of the Lord our strength,* we will not be able to resist the devil.

We were told *"Be sober, be vigilant; because your adversary the devil, as a roaring lion, walketh about, seeking whom he may devour:"* 1 Peter5:8. As long as you complain in life, you will always attract the devil into your life. Hear this, *"Neither murmur ye, as some of them also murmured, and were destroyed of the destroyer."* **1cor10:10**

Understanding God's Restoration Mandate

----*"For this is the will of God, even your sanctification, that ye should abstain from fornication:"* **1theo4:3**

If we must resist the devil we must stay away from sin. A life of sin is a life of wickedness. I life of sin is a life against the will and ordinances of God. *Do you want to serve God?* Then flea from sin. *"Now we know that God heareth not sinners: but if any man be a worshipper of God, and doeth his will, him he heareth."* **John9:31.**

I love for you to hear this…..

"Behold, the Lord's hand is not shortened, that it cannot save; neither his ear heavy that it cannot hear: But your iniquities have separated between you and your God, and your sins have hid his face from you, that he will not hear." **Isaia59:1-2**

CHAPTER 1 : God's Covenant of Abundance life

What are we saying?

The devil has been defeated over two thousand years ago. Just about anyone of us can do great things for the kingdom of God. I like for you to remain inspired, you will succeed in the midst of challenges. Most of the things we call obstacles are opportunities in disguise. I pray God grant you revelation and understanding to dominate and rule your world in Jesus Mighty Name.

I love to say that the answer to a man's prayer is an idea of what to do in life. There is a divine vision for you. I pray you encounter and discover it in your life time.

Whatever God is calling us to do, we must look for people who have done it in time past. It is written *"The thing that hath been, it is that which shall be; and that which is done is that which shall be done: and there is no new thing under the sun."* **Ecl1:9**

What I am saying is *for everyone to be persistent in your effort and desire to succeed in life.*

We must therefore *develop purpose, a goal, and a vision for your life and family.*

Always believe God that there is a way up, a way forward and a way out of any prevailing predicament. I can only encourage your life through the pages of this small book.

"It is written Whatsoever thy hand findeth to do, do it with thy might; for there is no work, nor device, nor knowledge, nor wisdom, in the grave, whither thou goest." **Eccl9:10**

"For even when we were with you, this we commanded you, that if any would not work, neither should he eat." **2theo3:10**

CHAPTER 1 : God's Covenant of Abundance life

"The sluggard will not plow by reason of the cold; therefore shall he beg in harvest, and have nothing." **Proverb20:4**

"He also that is slothful in his work is brother to him that is a great waster." **Proverb18:9**

"The soul of the sluggard desireth, and hath nothing: but the soul of the diligent shall be made fat." **Proverb13:4**

"He becometh poor that dealeth with a slack hand: but the hand of the diligent maketh rich." **Proverb10:4**

" For I know the plans I have for you," declares the LORD, "plans to prosper you and not to harm you, plans to give you hope and a future." **Jeremiah 29:11**

"One thing I ask from the LORD, this only do I seek: that I may dwell in the house of the LORD all the days of my life, to gaze on the beauty of the LORD and to seek him in his temple." **Psalm 27:4**

Understanding God's Restoration Mandate

"Taste and see that the LORD is good; blessed is the one who takes refuge in him." **Psalm 34:8**

"A friend loves at all times, and a brother is born for a time of adversity." **Proverbs 17:17**

"Greater love has no one than this: to lay down one's life for one's friends." **John 15:13**

"And we know that in all things God works for the good of those who love him, who have been called according to his purpose." **Romans 8:28**

"What, then, shall we say in response to these things? If God is for us, who can be against us?" **Romans 8:31**

"May the God of hope fill you with all joy and peace as you trust in him, so that you may overflow with hope by the power of the Holy Spirit." **Romans 15:13**

CHAPTER 1 : God's Covenant of Abundance life

"For I am convinced that neither death nor life, neither angels nor demons, neither the present nor the future, nor any powers, neither height nor depth, nor anything else in all creation, will be able to separate us from the love of God that is in Christ Jesus our Lord." **Romans 8:38-39**

"For now we see only a reflection as in a mirror; then we shall see face to face. Now I know in part; then I shall know fully, even as I am fully known." **1 Corinthians 13:12**

"Because of the LORD's great love we are not consumed, for his compassions never fail. They are new every morning; great is your faithfulness." **Lamentations 3:22-23**

"Therefore we do not lose heart. Though outwardly we are wasting away, yet inwardly we are being renewed day by day. 17 For our light and momentary troubles are achieving for us an eternal glory that far outweighs them all. So we fix our eyes not on what is seen, but on what is unseen, since what is seen is temporary, but what is unseen is eternal. **2 Corinthians 4:16-18**

"Be on your guard; stand firm in the faith; be courageous; be strong." **1 Corinthians 16:13**

PLEASE SAY THIS PRAYER AFTER ME.....

Say Lord Jesus, I am a sinner. I come to you surrendering all my wisdom, mighty, knowledge, and power. I give you glory. Use me Lord. Open thou my eyes that I may behold your word. Make a way for me where there seems to be no way. Lord do that which no man could have done. I vow to give you the glory the remaining day of my life. Thank you Jesus for saving me.

Amen

CHAPTER 2
GOD PRECIOUS PROMISES

"Whereby are given unto us exceeding great and precious promises: that by these ye might be partakers of the divine nature, having escaped the corruption that is in the world through lust."

2Peter1:4

In my search of the scriptures, I discovered seven precious promise that we must enjoy in life.

"Saying with a loud voice, Worthy is the Lamb that was slain to receive power, and riches, and wisdom, and strength, and honour, and glory, and blessing." **Rev5:12**

----------POWER----------

It is inevitable to for anyone to genuinely pray to God, without experiencing His majestic power. *"But ye shall receive power, after that the Holy Ghost is come upon you: and ye shall be witnesses unto me both in Jerusalem, and in all Judaea, and in Samaria, and unto the uttermost part of the earth."* **Acts1:8**

"Say unto God, How terrible art thou in thy works! through the greatness of thy power shall thine enemies submit themselves unto thee." **Psalms66:3**

"Behold, I give unto you power to tread on serpents and scorpions, and over all the power of the enemy: and nothing shall by any means hurt you."**Luke10:19**

CHAPTER 2 : God Precious Promises

----------RICHES----------

"Riches and honour are with me; yea, durable riches and righteousness." Proverb8:18.

"For there is no difference between the Jew and the Greek: for the same Lord over all is rich unto all that call upon him." **Romans10:12**

----------WISDOM----------

"I wisdom dwell with prudence, and find out knowledge of witty inventions." **Proverb8:12**

"Wisdom strengtheneth the wise more than ten mighty men which are in the city." **Eccl7:19**

Understanding God's Restoration Mandate

----------STRENGTH----------

"They go from strength to strength, every one of them in Zion appeareth before God." **Psalm 84:7**

"And there appeared an angel unto him from heaven, strengthening him." Luke22:43

----------HONOUR----------

"Riches and honour are with me; yea, durable riches and righteousness." Proverb8:18.

----------GLORY----------

"But we all, with open face beholding as in a glass the glory of the Lord, are changed into the same image from glory to glory, even as by the Spirit of the Lord."**2cor3:18.**

"And the glory of the Lord shall be revealed, and all flesh shall see it together:

CHAPTER 2 : God Precious Promises

for the mouth of the Lord hath spoken it." **Isaiah40:5**

"It is the glory of God to conceal a thing: but the honour of kings is to search out a matter." **Proverb25:2**

----------BLESSINGS----------

"The blessing of the Lord, it maketh rich, and he addeth no sorrow with it." Proverb10:22

Hindrances to the blessings of God

----------*Doubt*----------

As long as you doubt what God has done and will do, you hinder his blessing from manifesting upon your life.

It is written "A double minded man is unstable in all his ways." James1:8

----------Unbelief----------

I admonish you, believe God and you shall see his glory revealed upon your life. It is written "….Believe in the Lord your God, so shall ye be established; believe his prophets, so shall ye prosper." **2chronicle20:20**

One man said without a mentor, you are left in the hand of the tormentor. Talking about Jesus the bible says " And he could there do no mighty work, save that he laid his hands upon a few sick folk, and healed them. And he marvelled because of their unbelief. And he went round about the villages, teaching." **Mark6:5-6.**

----------Fear----------

"There were they in great fear, where no fear was: for God hath scattered the bones of him that encampeth against thee: thou

CHAPTER 2 : God Precious Promises

hast put them to shame, because God hath despised them" **Psalm 53:5**

What are you afraid of, there is no harm in trial. Fear of the unknown will deter anyone from take a bold step about their future."

Apostle Paul said "For a great door and effectual is opened unto me, and there are many adversaries." **1cor16:9**

----------*Sin*----------

"Behold, the Lord's hand is not shortened, that it cannot save; neither his ear heavy that it cannot hear: But your iniquities have separated between you and your God, and your sins have hid his face from you, that he will not hear." **Isaiah59:1-2**

"For sin shall not have dominion over you: for ye are not under the law, but under grace." **Romans6:14**

"If I regard iniquity in my heart, the Lord will not hear me." Psalms66:18

"Thy word have I hid in mine heart, that I might not sin against thee." **Psalm119:11**

Every time you are doing anything contrary to the will of God. Any action that contradicts the Holy Scripture and the commandment of the Lord. If you must succeed in life you must live right. If we must share our testimonies with others, we must do it scripturally.

"The soul that sinneth, it shall die. The son shall not bear the iniquity of the father, neither shall the father bear the iniquity of the son: the righteousness of the righteous shall be upon him, and the wickedness of the wicked shall be upon him." **Ezekiel18:20**

CHAPTER 2 : God Precious Promises

WE MUST REPENT OF OUR SINS

Wherefore seeing we also are compassed about with so great a cloud of witnesses, let us lay aside every weight, and the sin which doth so easily beset us, and let us run with patience the race that is set before us, **Hebrew12:1.**

We must not allow sin to destroy our calling and destiny in life. We must therefore repent of any known sin in our lives before God can restore our destiny.

For sin shall not have dominion over you: for ye are not under the law, but under grace. **Romans6:14**

Every time we yield to sin, we place ourselves in captivity. We must all strive to forsake sin and do away with every evil that dent our Christian dignity. Know ye not, that to whom ye yield yourselves servants to obey, his servants ye are to whom ye obey; whether of sin unto death, or of obedience unto righteousness? **Romans6:16**

It is written *"Be not overcome of evil, but overcome evil with good."* **Romans12:21**.We must all repent of any know sin that dents our Christian walk with the Lord Jesus Christ

How to I come out of sin?

Although we are all sinners, it takes *a will power* of the mind for us to repent and come out of sin. So many people and died because they could not let go the sin that easily best them go. Preacher who used to drug addicts have crashed and died because they went back into their addiction. A great man of God who repented because of alcohol in the family died of excessive alcohol abuse. We must make up our mind

CHAPTER 2 : God Precious Promises

for good if we must come out of sin. We must confess, and forsake it in the mighty name of Jesus.

The word says as many as received him, to them gave He power to become the sons of God. Even to them that believe on his name.

To qualify for divine visitation do the following sincerely

1) Acknowledge that you are a sinner and that He died for you. Rom3:23.

2) Repent of your sins. Acts 3:19, Luke13:5, 2Peter3:9

3) Believe in your heart that Jesus died for your sin. Romans10:10

4) Confess Jesus as the Lord over your life. Romans10:10, Acts2:21

Now repeat this Prayer after me

Say Lord Jesus, I accept you today, as my Lord and my savior, forgive me of my sins wash me with your blood. Right now, I believe, I am sanctified, I am save, I am free, I am free from the Power of sin to serve the Lord Jesus. Thank you Lord for saving me. Amen.

PRAYER POINT

"While men slept, his enemy came and sowed tares among the wheat, and went his way." **Matthew 13:25**

The midnight battle is a program designed by the Holy Ghost in order to arouse the Lord of Hosts to fight our battles and give us total victory.

Through this prayer session, God shall lift your head over the heads of your enemies. Follow the prayer session till the end, and your testimony shall give birth to multiple testimonies.

CHAPTER 2 : God Precious Promises

ANCHOR SCRIPTURE: PSALM 2

1. My Father, I am in your courtroom now, avenge me of my adversaries, in Jesus Name.
2. Domestic witchcraft, I drag you to the court of the Almighty, in Jesus Name.
3. My stubborn enemies, I drag you to the court of the Almighty, in Jesus Name.
4. Enemies of my progress, I drag you to the court of the Almighty, in Jesus Name.
5. God Arise! Judge them by fire! in Jesus Name.
6. Garment of darkness on my body, CATCH FIRE! in Jesus Name.
7. Power of environmental covens, Die, in Jesus Name.
8. Opportunity wasters, my life is not your candidate, Die! in Jesus Name.

Understanding God's Restoration Mandate

9. Any chain binding my finances, Break Now! in Jesus Name.
10. Spiritual powerlessness, Die! in Jesus Name.
11. Drinkers of blood and eaters of flesh, Hear the word of the Lord, DIE! in Jesus Name.
12. My inner-man RECEIVE FIRE! (Pray it like machine-gun by repeating it several times), in Jesus Name.
13. By the power that healed blind Bartemaeus, O God Arise! Heal me by Fire! in Jesus Name.
14. Power of infirmity, Die, in Jesus Name.
15. Inherited infirmities, you are a liar! Die! in Jesus Name.
16. Blood of Jesus, sanitize my blood, in Jesus Name.
17. Witchcraft-sponsored infirmities, BACK-FIRE! in Jesus Name.

CHAPTER 2 : God Precious Promises

18. Bondage of infirmities, B-R-E-A-K! in Jesus Name.

19. Curses of infirmity B-R-E-A-K! in Jesus Name.

20. Any power prolonging infirmity, DIE! in Jesus Name.

21. Eaters of flesh; Drinkers of blood, my life is not your candidate, therefore, DIE! in Jesus Name.

22. Arrows of infirmity assigned against my head, B-A-C-K-F-I-R-E! in Jesus Name.

23. Agents of infirmity from my food, Die! in Jesus Name.

24. My Father, You are the One who created times and seasons, and You put me here to operate, I thank You Father for bringing me here today, by the power of the Holy Ghost, I recover my destiny from the hands of the wicked. Father, as David cried unto You, so do

I cry today, that: Father, my times are in Your Hands deliver me from my wicked enemies. OH GOD ***ARISE AND RESCUE MY DESTINY FROM THE HANDS OF THE WICKED in Jesus Name.***

25. Every altar of darkness raised against me in the heavenlies, DIE! in Jesus Name. (Kill the altar of darkness).

26. Every problem programmed into my life from the heavenlies, DIE! in Jesus Name. Blood of Jesus, Wipe Out, the handwriting of darkness assigned against me in the heavenlies, in Jesus Name.

27. Every arrow fired against me from the heavenlies, B-A-C-K-F-I-R-E! in Jesus Name.

28. Every diviner assigned against me from the heavenlies, RUN MAD! in Jesus Name.

CHAPTER 2 : God Precious Promises

28. My Father! Arise! Fight for me Now! in Jesus Name.

29. Every power assigned to destroy my destiny, DIE! in Jesus Name.

30. Every power of frustration that pursued me last year, Your Time Is Up! DIE! in Jesus Name.

31. Every enemy of my promotion and advancement S-C-A-T-T-E-R in Jesus Name.

32. Every operation of darkness in my family line, DIE! in Jesus Name.

33. I shall have unstoppable advancement in Jesus Name.

34. This year, the wealth of the unbelievers shall be transferred to my bosom, in Jesus Name.

35. This year, my star shall arise and fall no more, in Jesus Name.

36. This year, men shall chase me around with blessings, in Jesus Name.

Understanding God's Restoration Mandate

37. I recover ten-fold all my wasted years, in Jesus Name.

38. Every power of the night programmed against my progress, S-C-A-T-T-E-R! in Jesus Name.

39. Mountain of affliction before me, S-C-A-T-T-E-R! in Jesus Name.

40. Every dream affliction, Die! in Jesus Name.

41. This year, men shall compete to favour me, in Jesus Name.

42. Every evil hand that shall point to my star this year, W-H-I-T-H-E-R! in Jesus Name.

43. Every satanic malpractice over my family, I cut you off! in Jesus Name.

44. Every power assigned to use my life as a dumping ground, C-A-T-C-H-F-I-R-E! in Jesus Name.

45. Every tree of failure of my father's house, Die! in Jesus Name.

CHAPTER 2 : God Precious Promises

46. Let God Arise and my enemies be scattered. Let God, My WALL OF JERICHO ASSIGNED AGAINST MY SUCCESS, S-C-A-T-T-E-R! in Jesus Name.

47. Every opposition against my possession, DIE! in Jesus Name.

48. Every tongue anointed by satan to speak against my life, You Are A LIAR! DIE! in Jesus Name.

49. Every power declaring that it is over for me, You Are A LIAR! DIE! in Jesus Name.

50. Every good thing that I have laid my hands upon, my hands shall finish it, in Jesus Name.

51. Every yoke upon my hands, B-R-E-A-K! in Jesus Name.

52. Any curse issued against my hands, B-R-E-A-K! in Jesus Name.

53. Thou power of poverty, DIE! in Jesus Name.
54. Thou power of bad luck, DIE! in Jesus Name.
55. Serpents of death; serpents of wastage, assigned against my hands, DIE! in Jesus Name.
56. Every strongman assigned against my hands, What Are You Waiting For? DIE! in Jesus Name.
57. Every evil power of my father's house assigned against my hands, DIE! in Jesus Name. (Lift up your two hands and wave it to the Lord, as u are waving those hands, every arrow of darkness upon the hands is being shaken out, every cobwebs and spirit of death and hell upon the hand are being taken out….)
58. Blood of Jesus, Arise in your POWER! ENVELOPE my hands! in Jesus Name.

CHAPTER 2: God Precious Promises

59. My hands shall bury bad things; it shall not bury good things, in Jesus Name.

60. Any power that has tied down my destiny, BREAK-LOOSE, from my life, in Jesus Name.

61. Wherever the stars have been programmed to disturb my destiny, O God Arise! Manifest your POWER! in Jesus Name.

62. Every witchcraft power toying with my destiny, DIE! in Jesus Name.

63. God of Elijah! ATTACK my red sea! in Jesus Name.

64. My Father! Reshuffle my environment to favour me! in Jesus Name. (Let there be a re-shuflement to favour me).

65. My Father! If I have been disconnected from the socket of my destiny, reconnect me by fire! in Jesus Name.

66. My Father, whatever you have not positioned into my life, wipe them off! in Jesus Name.

67. God Arise! And dismantle the poison in my foundation! in Jesus Name.

68. Negative circumstances that is affecting my success, BOW! in Jesus Name.

69. I curse the spirit of backwardness, in Jesus Name.

70. Every witchcraft register bearing my destiny, C-A-T-C-H-F-I-R-E! in Jesus Name.

71. Every power delaying the manifestation of my breakthroughs, DIE! in Jesus Name.

72. God Arise! And rearrange my circumstances to bring me into glory! in Jesus Name.

CHAPTER 2 : God Precious Promises

73. Every proclamation of the powers of darkness against my life, DIE! in Jesus Name.

74. God Arise! And package testimonies for me in Jesus Name.

75. Satanic decree working against my life, DIE! in Jesus Name. (Nullify the decree, cancel it).

76. Every calendar of the enemy, working against my life, CLEAR AWAY! in Jesus Name.

77. You evil programmers, let me go! in Jesus Name.

78. Anything programmed into my foundation to waste my destiny, DIE! in Jesus Name.

79. Any seasonal problem, programmed into my life, I de-programme you by fire! in Jesus Name.

80. You altar of evil programmers, assigned against my life, DIE! in Jesus Name.

81. My Father! If I have obeyed any evil command, KILL IT! in the name of Jesus.

82. Witchcraft programming; You are A LIAR! DIE! in the name of Jesus.

83. Any negative power, programmed against my head, JUMP OUT NOW! in the name of Jesus.

84. Satanic programming in the dream, Your Time Is Up! Therefore, DIE! in the name of Jesus.

85. Every witchcraft material planted into my life from the womb, DIE! in the name of Jesus.

86. In the Name of the King of kings, In the name of the Lord of lords, In the name of JESUSCHRIST! Every

CHAPTER 2 : God Precious Promises

witchcraft bondage in my life, B-R-E-A-K!

87. Any power calling my name into a cauldron, You Are A LIAR! DIE! in the name of Jesus.

88. Blood of Jesus, WIPE OFF every witchcraft name assigned against me, in the name of Jesus.

89. Every witchcraft padlock assigned against me, LOCK UP YOUR OWNER, in the name of Jesus.

90. Every astral projection against my life, BE ARRESTED! in the name of Jesus.

91. Every witchcraft power that have set eyes on me, RECEIVE BLINDNESS! in the name of Jesus.

92. Every witchcraft coven assigned against my destiny, S-C-A-T-T-E-R! in the name of Jesus.

93. Poverty stronghold, I cast u down, I set u ablaze! in the name of Jesus.

Understanding God's Restoration Mandate

94. Every power contesting for my oil, DIE! in the name of Jesus.

95. Every good thing stolen from my life by night, COME BACK NOW! in the name of Jesus.

96. Every good thing stolen from my life by the day, COME BACK! in the name of Jesus.

97. Arrows of the day, Arrows of the night assigned against my life, B-A-C-K-F-I-R-E! in the name of Jesus.

98. Every mouth of the wicked speaking against me, SHUT UP! in the name of Jesus.

99. Ministry of fear in my life, DIE! DIE!! DIE!!! in the name of Jesus.

100. Every power stealing my promotion, DIE! in the name of Jesus.

101. Every abnormal pattern in my family line, DIE! in the name of Jesus. [Pray this seven hot times]

CHAPTER 2 : God Precious Promises

102. God Arise and make me a wonder! in the name of Jesus.

103. Every power reporting me to witchcraft meetings, DIE! DIE!! DIE!!! in the name of Jesus.

104. Every meeting summoned to waste my life, in the name of Jesus.

105. Information about my life present on any wicked altar, C-A-T-C-H-F-I-R-E! in the name of Jesus.

106. Camera of darkness, taking my pictures in the dark world, C-A-T-C-H-F-I-R-E! in the name of Jesus.

107. Every inherited power assigned to waste my destiny, COME OUT NOW! In the name of Jesus.

108. Communication gadgets of darkness transferring my information, C-A-T-C-H-F-I-R-E! in the name of Jesus.

Understanding God's Restoration Mandate

109. Every agenda, Every programme, Every plan of darkness for my life, DIE! in the name of Jesus.

110. My wealth, buried in the earth, COME FORTH! in the name of Jesus.

111. Every arrow of witchcraft fired into my prosperity, DIE!!! in the name of Jesus.

112. Garment of poverty, C-A-T-C-H-F-I-R-E! in the name of Jesus.

113. You financial killer of my father's house, I am not your candidate! Therefore, DIE!!! in the name of Jesus.

114. Expected and unexpected financial breakthrough, LOCATE ME BY FIRE! in the name of Jesus.

115. Poverty activator dreams, Hear the word of the Lord! S-C-A-T-T-E-R! in the name of Jesus.

116. God Arise and use me to change my family history, in the name of Jesus.

CHAPTER 2 : God Precious Promises

117. My end shall be better than my beginning, in the name of Jesus.

118. Anything buried that is pulling me down, DIE! in the name of Jesus.

119. Oracles of my father's house, speaking against my progress, in the name of Jesus.

120. Power of collective captivity, my life is not your candidate, therefore, S-C-A-T-T-E-R! in the name of Jesus.

121. Parental curses, that is working against my life, CLEAR AWAY!!! in the name of Jesus.

122. I re-write my family history by the power in the blood of Jesus.

123. Any problem that came into my life through any dead relative, you are a liar, DIE!!! in the name of Jesus.

124. My life, reject wastage, in the name of Jesus.

125. Every agenda of the enemy to capture my spirit-man, FAIL! in the name of Jesus.

126. Spirit of perdition, spirit of perverseness, LOOSE YOUR HOLD, upon my life, in the name of Jesus.

127. Every power tying me down to iniquity, B-R-E-A-K-A-W-A-Y!!! in the name of Jesus.

128. Hell fire shall not harvest my life, in the name of Jesus.

129. My Father, if I am presently wrongly scheduled, RESCHEDULE ME! in the name of Jesus.

130. The enemy would not write the last chapter of my life, in the name of Jesus.

131. Every evil master, rejoicing at my sadness, DIE! in the name of Jesus.

132. Every power drawing my virtues, You are a LIAR! DIE! in the name of Jesus.

CHAPTER 2 : God Precious Promises

133. My transferred blessings, hear the word of the Lord, C-O-M-E B-A-C-K!!! in the name of Jesus.

134. Every padlock holding down my progress, C-A-T-C-H-F-I-R-E! in the name of Jesus.

135. Spiritual robbers in my habitation, LOOSE YOUR POWER!!! in the name of Jesus.

136. [For Sisters only] Satanic agents wearing my wedding garments, Take It OFF by Fire! in the name of Jesus.

137. [For Brothers Only] Power of hard labour, DIE!!! in the name of Jesus.

138. Merchants of souls, assigned against my destiny, DIE! in the name of Jesus.

139. My heavens OPEN! My rain of blessing FALL!! in the name of Jesus.

140. My Father, do anything to turn my life around, in the name of Jesus.

141. Commanded blessings! Overtaking Blessings!! Added Blessings!!! APPEAR IN MY LIFE!!! in the name of Jesus.

142. God of the turn-around, I am here, LOCATE ME NOW! in the name of Jesus.

143. Star Hunters, assigned against me, DIE! in the name of Jesus.

144. Powers assigned to make my life useless, DIE! in the name of Jesus.

145. My breakthroughs from the four corners of the earth, LOCATE ME NOW! in the name of Jesus.

146. Any power disconnecting me from the virtues of the Lord, DIE! in the name of Jesus.

147. My lost FIRE! COME BACK!!! in the name of Jesus.

CHAPTER 2 : God Precious Promises

148. Powers assigned to push me to the back, E-X-P-I-R-E!!! in the name of Jesus.

149. In my dream life, My Father, APPEAR!!! in the name of Jesus.

150. My eyes OPEN! SEE the Lord!! in the name of Jesus.

151. What stopped my father, will not stop me! in the name of Jesus.

152. Power of limitation, you are a LIAR! DIE!!! in the name of Jesus.

153. I dismantle every power of backwardness, in the name of Jesus.

154. Every power assigned to disorganize my life, DIE! in the name of Jesus.

155. My hands Receive power to prosper, in the name of Jesus.

156. My Father, rearrange my circumstances to catapult my life, in the name of Jesus.

CONCLUSION

"And I will restore to you the years that the locust hath eaten, the cankerworm, and the caterpiller, and the palmerworm, my great army which I sent among you." **Joel 2:25**

"And ye shall eat in plenty, and be satisfied, and praise the name of the Lord your God, that hath dealt wondrously with you: and my people shall never be ashamed." **Joel 2:26**

"And ye shall know that I am in the midst of Israel, and that I am the Lord your God, and none else: and my people shall never be ashamed." **Joel 2:27**

"Restore unto me the joy of thy salvation; and uphold me with thy free spirit." **Psalms 51:12**

"Therefore if any man be in Christ, he is a new creature: old things are passed

CHAPTER 2 : God Precious Promises

away; behold, all things are become new". 2cor5:17

Are you a sinner or a born again believer?

What must I do to determine my divine visitation?

To determine divine visitation you must be born again. The word says as many as received him, to them gave He power to become the sons of God. Even to them that believe on his name.

To qualify for divine visitation do the following sincerely

1) Acknowledge that you are a sinner and that He died for you.Rom3:23.

2) Repent of your sins. Acts 3:19, Luke13:5, 2Peter3:9

3) Believe in your heart that Jesus died for your sin.Romans10:10

Understanding God's Restoration Mandate

4) Confess Jesus as the Lord over your life. Romans10:10, Acts2:21

Now repeat this Prayer after me

Say Lord Jesus, I accept you today, as my Lord and my savior, forgive me of my sins wash me with your blood. Right now, I believe, I am sanctified, I am save, I am free, I am free from the Power of sin to serve the Lord Jesus. Thank you Lord for saving me. Amen.

Have you suffered a setback?

God want to restore your life beyond your wildest imagination.

Have you been through a divorce?

God want to give a relationship that is exactly the desire of your heart.

CHAPTER 2 : God Precious Promises

Did your lost business or money?

God want to bless you more than you have before.

"So the Lord blessed the latter end of Job more than his beginning: for he had fourteen thousand sheep, and six thousand camels, and a thousand yoke of oxen, and a thousand she asses." Job42:12

WISDOM KEYS

Every Productive Society is a society heading to the top

Millions of Nigerians run away from Nigeria, very few Nigerians stay in Nigeria.

My decision to return Nigeria is the will of God for my life

My short coming in America after 18 years, trained me to be wise, to think, reflect and reason appropriately.

If you train your mind to reason it will train your hands to earn money.

It is absurd to use the money of the heathen to build the kingdom of the living God.

Every Ministry reveals its agenda and goal either at the beginning or at the end. Be careful of your life it is your first Ministry.

The average American mind is conditioned for a continual quest to get new things and (discard the former) and throw away old things.

When I considered well, my BMW jeep became my initial deposit for the work of the ministry in Nigeria.

Everyone is waiting for you to change your mind until you change your thinking nothing changes around you.

CHAPTER 2 : God Precious Promises

Multiple academic degrees in other discipline gave me the chance to think, reflect, and reason

What so everyone are thinking and reflecting at the moment reveals you to the time and the now factor

All events and intents are the product of precise thought processes, accurate reason every event is designed for a designated timeline

Wisdom is your ability to think, to create and invent. If you can think wise enough you will come out of penury

The distance between you and success is your creative ability to think reason and reflect accurate.

Success is the result of hard work, commitment resolve, and determination learning from past mistakes and failing.

If you organize your mind you have organized your life and destiny.

There is a thin line between success and failure. If you look above and beyond you are on your way to success.

Wealth is your ability to think, power is your ability to reason and success is your ability to be informed.

If you can make use of your mind by thinking and reasoning God will make use of your life and destiny.

Think and Be Great

Reflect, Reason, think and be great

Famous people are born of woman

That you will make it is your intention; that you will survive is your resolve, that you will succeed with changes is your determination, personal efforts and hard work.

CHAPTER 2 : God Precious Promises

No man was born a failure. Lack of vision is the end product of failure.

Working with mental patients encourages and aspire me to be a productive observant and dedicated to my assignment.

Successful people are not magicians, it is the will power combined with hard work, and determination and a resolve to succeed that make them succeed.

In the unequivocal state of the mind, intention is not a location or a position it is the state of the mind.

So many people think that they think. The mind is used to think reflect and reason. You will remain blind with your eye open until you can see with your mind by thinking.

There is no favoritism in accurate and precise calculation

Understanding God's Restoration Mandate

Although knowledge is power, information is the key and gateway to a great future.

It will take the hand of God to move the hand of man.

With the backing of the great wise God, nothing will disconnect you from your inheritance.

As long as you have wisdom and understanding of God, Satan and evil cannot manipulate your life and destiny.

You have come this far by yourself judgment and decision you have made in the past, now lean and listen to God for another dimension of greatness.

Great people are common people it is extra ordinary effort and the price of sacrifice that produces greatness.

CHAPTER 2 : God Precious Promises

As a mental direct care worker I saw a great pastor and a motivational speaker within myself.

Menial job does not reduce your self-worth, until you resolve to achieve greatness see greatness in all you do; you will never count in your community.

The principle of Jesus will solve your gambling and addiction problems

The man of Jesus will lead you into heaven,

Everyone have their self-appraisal and what they think about you. Until you discover yourself other opinion about you will alter the real you.

Supervisors and directors are just a position in the chain of command in a work place. Never allow your supervisor hierarchy to alter your opinion about yourself.

Understanding God's Restoration Mandate

Everyone can come out of debt if they make up their mind.

That I am not a decision maker at work does not diminish my contribution to my world.

Although it appears like it was a poor decision to accept a direct care employment at a psychiatric hospital as I reflect of my nine years of experience, it became apparent that I have learnt and experienced enough for my next assignment.

Self-encouragement and determination is a resolve of the heart.

If you are determined to make a difference, and do the things that make a difference you will eventually make a difference.

Good things do not come easy

Short cuts will cut your life short.

CHAPTER 2 : God Precious Promises

Those who look ahead move ahead.

Life is all about making an impact. In your life time strive to make an impact in your community.

Make friends and connect with people who are moving ahead of you in life.

If you can look around well you have come a long way in your life, made a lot of difference and realized a lot of success in life.

If you are my old friend, hurry up to reach out to me before I become a stranger to you.

Everything I am blessed with inspirations from God, that change my definition and interpretation of the world around me.

I thought I was stagnant and lonely until I looked around and noticed my children running around and my wife cooking.

Understanding God's Restoration Mandate

At 40 I resigned my Job to seek the Lord forever.

My ministry took a drastic rise to the top when the wisdom of God visited me with knowledge and understanding.

You will be a better person if you understand the characteristics of your personality – your mood swings attitudes and habits.

It is the seed of love you sow into the heart of a child and a woman that you reap in due time.

Love is not selfish, love share everything including the concealed secrets of the mind.

As long as you have a prayer life and a bible; you will never feel lonely, rejected, and idle in the race of life.

When good friends disconnect from you, let them go, they might have seen something new in a different direction.

CHAPTER 2 : God Precious Promises

Confidence in yourself and in God is the only way to bring you out of captivity

Never train a child to waste his/her time.

The mind is the greatest assets of a great future.

You walk by common sense run by principles and fly by instruction.

Those who fly in flight of life fly alone.

I have seen a tolling vehicle I have seen a tolling ship I have never seen a tolling airplane.

I exercise my judgment and make a decision every minute of the day.

Decisions are crucial, critical, and vital with reference to your future.

So many people wish for a great future. You can only work towards a great future.

Your celebrity status began when you discovered your talent. What are you good at? Work at it with all commitment.

Prayers will sustain you but the wisdom of God will prosper you.

When I met Oyedepo, his teachings changed my perspective, but

when I met Ibiyeomie; His teaching changed my perception.

I will be successful in ministry if only I concentrate and focus my energy in the work of the ministry.

It took the late Dr. Vincent Pearle Norman's book to open my mind towards kingdom success.

CHAPTER 4
PRAYER OF SALVATION

"Neither is there salvation in any other: for there is none other name under heaven given among men, whereby we must be saved." Acts 4:12.

The purpose of this small book will be defeated if you finish reading without hearing a message about your salvation. Hear me out! Your sanctification, and Salvation is very important to God, and to your soul.

Are you saved?

To be saved we must be born again! The word says as many as received him, to them gave He power to become the sons of God. Even to them that believe on his name.

Understanding God's Restoration Mandate

To qualify for divine visitation do the following sincerely

1) Acknowledge that you are a sinner and that He died for you.Rom3:23.

2) Repent of your sins. Acts 3:19, Luke13:5, 2Peter3:9

3) Believe in your heart that Jesus died for your sin.Romans10:10

4) Confess Jesus as the Lord over your life. Romans10:10, Acts2:21

Now repeat this Prayer after me

Say Lord Jesus, I accept you today, as my Lord and my savior, forgive me of my sins wash me with your blood. Right now, I believe, I am sanctified, I am save, I am free, I am free from the Power of sin to serve the Lord Jesus. Thank you Lord for saving me. Amen. Congratulation: YOU ARE NOW A BORN AGAIN CHRISTAIN

CHAPTER 4 : Prayer of Salvation

AGAIN I SAY TO YOU CONGRATULATION

I adjure you to watch the Spirit of God bear witness with your Spirit confirming His word with signs following. The word says The Spirit itself beareth witness with our spirit, that we are the children of God.

MIRACLE CARE OUTREACH

"…But that the members should have the same care one for another" 1cor12:25

We are all members of the body of Christ. Jesus commanded us to love our neighbor as ourselves. This includes caring for one another as a member of one body. True love is expressed in caring and giving. The word says for God so Love He gave….

Reach out to someone in need of Jesus, help someone in crisis find Christ. Look out and prove your love to Jesus by caring and inviting your friends and associates to find Jesus the Healer.

Invite your friends to our Home Care Cell Fellowship (Miracle chapel Intl Satellite fellowship) In the USA at 33 Schley Street Newark New Jersey 07112.

If you are in Nigeria—**MIRACLE OF GOD MINISTRIES**

A.K.A"**MIRACLE CHAPEL INTL**" Mpama –Egbu-Owerri Imo state Nigeria.

(Home Care Cell fellowship Group).We meet every Tuesday at 6:00pm-7:00pm.

LIFE IS NOT ALL ABOUT DURATION BUT ITS ALL ABOUT DONATION

What does the above statement mean?….

Life consists not in accumulation of material wealth..Luke12:15. But it's all

CHAPTER 4 : Prayer of Salvation

about liberality….meaning- what you can give and share with others. Proverb11:25. When you live for others--You live forever- because you out live your generation by the legacy you live behind after you depart into glory to be with the Lord. But when you live to yourself - you are reduced to self—you are easily forgotten when you die and depart in glory. Permit me to admonish you today to live your life to be a blessing to a soul connected to you today. I want you to know that so many souls are connected and looking up to you, and through you so many souls will be saved and rescued from destruction. Will you disciple someone today to find Jesus Christ?

As a genuine Christian; it is your duty to evangelize Jesus Christ to all you meet on your way. Jesus is still in the healing business-Jesus is still doing miracles from time of old to now. Therefore tell someone about Jesus Christ today, disciple and bring them to Church. John 1:45 Philip findeth Nathanael....

Please to prove the sincerity of your love for God today; please become a soul winner. The dignity of your Christianity is hidden in your boldness to proclaim and evangelize Jesus Christ to all you meet on your way. There is a question mark on the integrity of your Christianity until you become a life soul winner. Invite someone to join us worship the Lord Jesus this coming Sunday. **Amen**

MIRACLE OF GOD MINISTRIES PILLARS OF THE COMMISSION

We Believe Preach and Practice the following

1) We believe and preach Salvation to every living human being

2) We believe and preach Repentance and forgiveness of sins

CHAPTER 4 : Prayer of Salvation

3) We believe and preach the baptism of the Holy Spirit and Spiritual gifts

4) We believe and teach the Prosperity

5) We believe and preach Divine Healing and Miracles (Signs &Wonder)

6) We believe and preach Faith

7) We believe and Proclaim the Power of God (Supernatural)

8) We believe and Proclaim Praise& Worship to God

9) We believe and preach Wisdom

10) We believe and preach Holiness (Consecration)

11) We believe and preach Vision

12) We believe and teach the Word of God

13) We believe and teach Success

14) We believe and practice Prayer

15) We believe and teach Deliverance

Understanding God's Restoration Mandate

This 15 stones form the Pillars of Our Commission. Become part of this church family and follow this great move of God.

MY HEART FELT PRAYER FOR YOU

The truth is that; God want us restored and be blessed. I love for you to embrace my restoration prayer for you. You might have lost your entire business, money and marriage but I guarantee you, God is about to do strange wonders in your life. If you believe that please join me by repeating this short prayer below

Now let me Pray for you:

Lord Jesus, I thank you for you are still in the restoration business. Father restore everything I ever lost as a result of ignorant,

CHAPTER 4 : Prayer of Salvation

shame carelessness fear or doubt. I thank you for what you have done. But I praise you for what you will do for us even now. In Jesus Mighty Name. Amen

CHAPTER 4
ABOUT THE AUTHOR

Rev Franklin N Abazie is the founding and Presiding Pastor of Miracle of God Ministries with headquarters in Newark, New Jersey USA and a branch church in Owerri- Imo State Nigeria. He is following the footsteps of one of his mentors, Oral Roberts (Healing Evangelist) of the blessed memory. The Lord passed Oral Roberts healing mantle two days before he went to be with the Lord at age 91 into the hand of healing evangelist-Rev Franklin N Abazie in a vision.

In all his services the Power and Presence of God is present to heal all in his audience. He is an ordained man of God with a Healing Ministry reviving the healing

Chapter 4 : ABOUT THE AUTHOR

and miracle ministry of Jesus Christ of Nazareth.

Pastor Franklin N Abazie, is called by God with a unique mandate: **"THE MOMENT IS DUE TO IMPACT YOUR WORLD THROUGH THE REVIVAL OF THE HEALING & MIRACLE MINISTRY OF JESUS CHRIST OF NAZARETH**

I AM SENDING YOU TO RESTORE HEALTH UNTO THEE AND I WILL HEAL THEE OF THY WOUNDS. SAID THE LORD OF HOST"

He is a gifted ardent Teacher of the word of God who operates also in the office of a Prophet, generating and attracting undeniable signs & wonders, special miracles and healings, with apostolic fireworks of the Holy Ghost. He is the founding and presiding senior Pastor of this fast growing Healing ministry. He has written over 86 inspirational, healing and transforming books covering almost all aspect of divine healing and life. He is happily married and blessed with children.

BOOKS BY REV FRANKLIN N ABAZIE

1) Commanding Abundance
2) The Outcome of faith
3) Understanding the secret of prevailing prayers.
4) Understanding the secret of the man God uses
5) Activating my due Season
6) Overcoming Divine Verdicts
7) The Outcome of Divine Wisdom
8) Understanding God's Restoration Mandate
9) Walking in the Victory and Authority of the truth
10) Gods Covenant Exemption
11) Destiny Restoration Pillars
12) Provoking Acceptable Praise
13) Understanding Divine Judgment

14) Activating Angelic Re-enforcement
15) Provoking Un-Merited Favor
16) The Benefits of the Speaking faith
17) Understanding Divine Arrangement
18) Understanding Divine Healing
19) The Mystery of Endurance
20) Obeying Divine Instructions
21) Understanding the Voice of God
22) Never give up on Hope
23) The prevailing Power of faith
24) Understanding Divine Prosperity
25) The Reward of Prayer
26) Covenant Keys to Answered Prayers
27) Activating the Forces of Vengeance
28) Put your faith to work
29) Where is your trust?
30) The Audacity of the Blood of Jesus
31) Redeeming Your Days
32) The Force of Vision

33) Breaking the shackles of Family curses
34) Wisdom for Marriage Stability
35) Overcoming prevailing challenges
36) The Prayer solution
39) The power of Prayer
40) The effective strategy of Prayer
41) The prayer that works
42) Walking in Forgiveness
43) The power of the grace of God
44) The power of Persistence
45) The prevailing power of the blood of Jesus
46) The Benefit of the speaking faith.
47) Fearless faith
48) Redeeming Your Days.
49) The Supernatural Power of Prophecy
50) The companionship of the Holy Spirit
51) Understanding Divine Prosperity
52) Dominating Controlling Forces

53) The winner's Faith
54) Developing Spiritual Muscles
55) Inexplicable faith
56) The lifestyle of Prayer
57) Developing a positive attitude in life.
58) The mystery of Divine supply
59) Encounter with the Power of God
60) Walking in love
61) Praying in the Spirit
62) How to provoke your testimony
63) Walking in the reality of the anointing
64) The reality of new birth
65) The price of freedom
66) The Supernatural power of faith
67) The intellectual components of Redemption.
68) Overcoming Fear
69) Overcoming Prevailing Challenges
70) My life & Ministry

Books By Rev Franklin N Abazie

71) The Mystery of Praise
72) The Power of Bold Declaration
73) The Joy of Christmas
74) The prevailing Power of hope
75) The lifestyle of Praise
76) Commanding Faith
77) Dream Big & Believe in your self
78) The Power of Divine Intervention
79) The Power of Discipline & Dedication

MIRACLE OF GOD MINISTRIES
NIGERIA CRUSADE
2012

MIRACLE OF GOD MINISTRIES

NIGERIA CRUSADE 2012

MIRACLE OF GOD MINISTRIES

*NIGERIA CRUSADE
2012*

Wisdom Center
Forth-Worth Tex
Pastors Conferer
2017

www.ingramcontent.com/pod-product-compliance
Lightning Source LLC
Chambersburg PA
CBHW021128300426
44113CB00006B/331